Be Sure to Pick Up the Pearls

Reflections on Life

David Harris

BALBOA.
PRESS
A DIVISION OF HAY HOUSE

Balboa Press books may be ordered through booksellers or by contacting:

Balboa Press
A Division of Hay House
1663 Liberty Drive
Bloomington, IN 47403
www.balboapress.com
1 (877) 407-4847

Because of the dynamic nature of the Internet, any web addresses or
links contained in this book may have changed since publication and
may no longer be valid. The views expressed in this work are solely those
of the author and do not necessarily reflect the views of the publisher,
and the publisher hereby disclaims any responsibility for them.

The author of this book does not dispense medical advice or prescribe the use
of any technique as a form of treatment for physical, emotional, or medical
problems without the advice of a physician, either directly or indirectly. The
intent of the author is only to offer information of a general nature to help
you in your quest for emotional and spiritual well-being. In the event you use
any of the information in this book for yourself, which is your constitutional
right, the author and the publisher assume no responsibility for your actions.

Any people depicted in stock imagery provided by Thinkstock are models,
and such images are being used for illustrative purposes only.
Certain stock imagery © Thinkstock.

Printed in the United States of America.

ISBN: 978-1-4525-9023-3 (sc)
ISBN: 978-1-4525-9024-0 (hc)
ISBN: 978-1-4525-9022-6 (e)
Library of Congress Control Number: 2014900160

Balboa Press rev. date: 2/13/2014

Contents

Foreword

When I was first asked to write the foreword to this book, I wasn't sure whether I should accept. After all, I thought, shouldn't the foreword be composed by a great teacher or least a good writer? Might my own contribution be far too personal? For in addition to being a close friend and spiritual mentor, David Harris is also my father. Not *my father* in some abstract, spiritual sense, but my actual father.

In so many ways the support and inspiration I've received from this man is not unlike that received by countless others: friends, family, and clients who have come to rely on him for guidance, wisdom, and the warm friendship he generously offers to all. I can't count the times that some simple phrase uttered or humble words of wisdom offered (perhaps shared with a smile or laugh) has dropped like a potent seed into the soil of my consciousness, only to expand into some deeper way of understanding an important issue I had wrestled with over time. In my own years of exploring the depths of the great meaning of life, I've come to know, without any doubt, that this man stands among the few great teachers of my life.

As Socrates philosophized, "The unexamined life is not worth living." Nothing could be a truer expression of the moment-to-moment inquiry that has always marked my father's examination of life's deeper meanings. More than most people I've known, he approaches each day as an opportunity to see beneath the surface of things. Coincidences, happenstance, and accidents give way under his discerning eye, revealing synchronicities, gifts, and miracles.

Because of this practiced ability to see the extraordinary in the seemingly ordinary, he is able to extract pearls of insight from the churning sands of moment-to-moment existence. Those insights have illumined not only his own life but those of us who have been fortunate enough to know him as a counselor, a mentor, a friend, or in my case, a son. In these writings he invites us to pick up those same pearls or perhaps to find a few of our own as we learn to look at life outside the ordinary lens of everyday connection.

This book is so much more than the musings of one man sharing his own life lessons. It's an invitation to pay more careful attention to the beauty and possibility of every moment. It asks that each one of us more fully and vibrantly participate in the miracle of our own precious and unique existence. Indeed, the examined life is very much worth living.

Jeffrey Harris

Preface
Lessons Learned

As I have progressed through my life (I am eighty-five), I have had many experiences and have gained some wisdom. I say some wisdom because I am sure there are more lessons ahead. Because of my age, I have had many beautiful experiences and gifts, and many that were perhaps not so beautiful. In my article about wisdom in this book, I address the issue that wisdom can only be gained through experience. This book is based on both the heeded and unheeded lessons of my life. It is my hope that the lessons described in this book may assist some of my readers in this process of acquiring wisdom of their own.

David Harris

Chapter 1
Be Sure to Pick Up the Pearls

Have you ever wondered if we are guided in our lives by a force that helps direct our journey? Sometimes in my own life I've been struck by circumstances and phenomena that seem to speak to me with hidden messages, reminders that there is a deeper connection between the universe and myself.

These messages might appear large or small. Perhaps I'll think of someone I hadn't spoken to in years, and within an hour he or she will call. Or suddenly circumstances in my life unexpectedly change, creating the perfect opportunity to answer my urgent prayer. At other times a simple smile from a stranger or a sudden revelation about one's life can feel like part of a conspiracy to wake me up to a web of seemingly invisible connectivity. I can't help but sense at times that the universe itself seems to be having a conversation with us, asking us to take more notice and enticing us to pay attention to the everyday wonders.

It's easy to miss these miracles, to believe them to be meaningless fabrications of our own imagination. Picture yourself walking down a beach, watching the waves and the birds flying by but failing to notice the many beautiful and valuable pearls lying in the sand by your feet. These seemingly meaningless coincidences, answers to our prayers, and daily miracles are those pearls that we step over without noticing, without stopping to pick them up.

Earlier in my life it was rare that I would bend down to pick up one of these pearls, and even then I usually would discard it as a coincidence. I found that these pearls were scarce and hardly ever presented themselves to me.

And then, for no reason that I could think of, I noticed that I was finding more and more pearls. What was the change? How was it that the more pearls I found and picked up, the more pearls presented themselves to me to be found? The difference was that I began to see the deeper meaning and significance of each of these pearls. I began to literally polish them and put them on the shelf instead of discarding them. I could no longer ignore them as I came to see the significance of them in my life.

I believe that these pearls are placed in our paths when we need them most, as if sent as lessons from a higher power meant to aid us and guide us on our paths.

Watch for these pearls. They are there. They were there for me. Experiencing just one of them could be a life-changing event.

Chapter 2
Where Did the Child Go?

We don't stop playing because we grow old,
We grow old because we stop playing
(George Bernard Shaw, Biography)

Anд what are things that children do that make them children? Most importantly they play. They can act childish and goofy, they do not wear costumes of who they are not, they can ooh and ah at the zoo, they will feed the ducks at the park, and much more.

What are some of the things that grown-ups do? Sadly, they often feel that they must act grown-up. They often wear costumes of who they feel they are supposed to be. They are often not in the present, but may be engrossed in past regrets or future worries.

Play is vital to all adults. And play is whatever play is to you. It can be hollering at a football game or feeding the ducks. The key is to be totally in the present moment in some joyful fashion. Yes, we grown-ups do have to worry about paying rent, buying food and car insurance, and much more. But if this need consumes us and we do not make time to play in some fashion, the stress imposed on us by our culture can be costly in terms of health and longevity.

With the pressures of everyday life, I believe that it is most important to make space in our lives for the child that once was. It is about choosing to take off that grown-up costume and be the child who plays once again.

Chapter 3
Ego, the Big Cover
Are You Wearing a Costume?

E*go,* as defined by *Webster's Collegiate Dictionary Ninth Version,* is the following: the self as contrasted with another self or the world. In our everyday lives, we might see it as individuals more involved with themselves than others. And we all have aspects of this in our personalities or we could not be who we are.

Who we believe ourselves to be, and the value that we attribute to *me,* has a huge impact on the way we relate to everything and everyone else. A positive sense of oneself or high self-esteem allows us to interact with others in this world without the need *to wear a costume* or project some concocted image of who we want others to believe we are.

When negative self-images lead to a feeling of separation and fear, we are more and more likely to live in our costumes, pretending to be who we are not. There are many ways that this process becomes apparent. At one end of the spectrum is being a pleaser, where one may neglect his or her own needs in order to gain acceptance.

At the other end of the spectrum is the kind of person who needs to swagger around with what appears to be an overly inflated ego, appearing to have an out-of-proportion sense of self-importance. We have all encountered people like this in our lives.

This person who seems to have a need to show power can often make us feel *less than* in his or her need to control. This personality may appear confident and strong, but if we look beneath the surface we might notice that this person does not actually like him or herself as much as it appears. This costume may be just a cover to hide a deeper sense of fear and uncertainty. Studies in present-day psychology confirm the fact that low self-esteem is a major factor in an out-of-proportion sense of self-importance. This is the big cover-up.

If you were to call this person on such egocentric behavior, his or her normal defense would be to deny. More often than not, this individual would not even be aware of the possibility that his or her behavior is part of an elaborately created costume.

What might one do in the face of someone with what may be an overly inflated ego? First of all, in the face of any put downs or barbs, it's crucial to remember who you really *are*. One must wear the armor of self-love so that verbal attacks cannot get through. And secondly, remember the little boy or little girl who may be inside that egotistical costume. If at all possible, treat that person with love and respect, no matter how difficult that can be.

And how do we recognize our own costume, if in indeed we are wearing one? It is much more difficult to see this in ourselves. This subtle psychological veneer is a product of all of the factors in our lives that have made us who we are today. The major challenge in the process of true self-healing is in how to uncover one's own cover.

Are we truly who we believe we are? If our life is working, if we enjoy deep and trusting relationships, and if we are happy much of the time, then it is likely that we are living from our authentic self. However, when our life does not work, when we find ourselves in constant conflict with others and lack the experience of love and joy in our day-to-day existence, then it may be time to really look within.

This kind of self-inquiry can be challenging. The easiest thing is to blame others for our condition. But that Band-Aid will not work in the long run. It takes a true hero to look within one's own being, past what might be a falsely created costume, to find one's true self.

The ultimate reward of this search is to find the real you and the peace that follows its discovery. This simple authenticity in turn becomes the foundation for true and meaningful relationships.

Then truly, no costume is required.

Chapter 4
Don't Ask How

Some of us may have heard a story that goes like this: A man arrived in heaven after having drowned when his small boat sank in very bad weather. He asked God, "Why did you not answer my prayers when I was in trouble?" To which God answered, "Do you remember when a man warned you not to go to sea because of bad weather, and you said, 'God will take care of me'? Or when some men on a boat tried to rescue you, and you said, 'God will take care of me'? And when a helicopter tried to rescue you, you said, 'God will take care of me.'" God then continued, "What more could I have done?"

I had a similar experience. My brother and I were sailplane pilots, and we had gone to a sailplane event in Minden, Nevada. One evening we had parked our car and when we returned two hours later, the engine would not start due to a dead battery. We made several unsuccessful phone calls to the local auto club to get help. We felt quite helpless in a strange town. I have been a practicing energy healer for many years, so I decided to use my skills in restarting the engine from a dead battery. I placed my hands on the hood of the car and asked my brother to hit the starter, intending and expecting the engine to start. However, at the very instant that I asked my brother to hit the starter, a truck from the local auto club (which we had never been able to reach) pulled up, and the driver said something like, "Are you guys having trouble, and can I help?" And with his help, the car was started. A truly miraculous occurrence, I thought. But certainly not done in any way that I might have intended or even imagined. I feel that it was not unlike the story of the man who drowned when his boat sank and he asked God for help.

Bottom line, when a miracle occurs, don't ask how—just accept it.

Chapter 5
Live Your Life with Passion

You might ask, "Why should I live my life with passion?" What is there to be passionate about? Most importantly it could add a dimension of aliveness and richness to your life that you might never have been able to imagine.

The word *passion* has many synonyms, some of which are excitement, enthusiasm, joy, fervor, or zeal. The opposite of passion would be boredom, tiresome, dullness, or monotony. Which words fit your life?

The first step is to make a decision to do whatever is necessary to bring more of this lovely quality into your life. It is about changing your attitude in a positive and joyful way in as many areas of your life as is possible. Being passionate can become a habit. And for sure there are areas of everyone's life that are far beyond this Pollyanna approach.

Look at your work, your hobbies, your partner, the clouds in the sky, your children, your friends, the beauty of nature, and so on. Notice any areas that seem to ignite you, and then focus on them and savor them. Rekindle these thoughts whenever a funk strikes.

If you cannot find such a place, then create it. It could involve joining an organization, finding a hobby, or any one of a multitude of other possibilities that might turn you on in a passionate fashion.

I have asked myself, when am I most happy? After much consideration I realized that it was when I was doing something about which I was most passionate, whether it is something as simple as holding my wife's hand or building a wooden boat. It may be a challenge, but the rewards are well worth it.

Chapter 6
Be Careful, It's Contagious

Have you ever been in a funk, and someone walks by and throws you a cheerful "Hi" with a smile, and your mood changes in the blink of an eye? Or have you ever been in a down mood, and then you walk into the presence of a bunch of *up* people and you can seem to catch their up mood?

Another example would be when the head of your place of business is an up person—that vibe seems to affect everyone in the organization. Unfortunately, when that person is negative, the aura of the whole organization can also move in that negative direction.

What I am presenting here is that I believe that conditions such as happiness, compassion, kindness, optimism, contentment, and innumerable other human traits are transmissible or contagious, almost like the common cold.

I am suggesting is that there is a real form of energy that connects all things, including emotions. It is real, and it manifests itself in innumerable ways in our everyday lives. Such things as the vibe between people, cultures, animals, and even plants may be just one of the many manifestations of this phenomenon.

The name assigned by some branches of science to this phenomenon is Subtle Energy. I am speaking about another dimension, which just now is being investigated by Western science, even though it may have existed forever. It is so obvious that no one seems to notice it. It is like no one noticed gravity until Newton discovered it.

An example of how this vibe of happiness might spread through a culture would be Denmark, which is known to be the happiest of all countries. What I am suggesting is that this subtle energy phenomenon may be the means by which happiness may have spread through this country like a benign infection.

Assuming that my suppositions are true, how can we in our own lives benefit from these hypotheses? For one thing, just be aware of this subtle energy and watch how it operates. Hang only with positive people. Be cautious of people that are chronically negative, because this also can infect you. Notice how your level of happiness and contentment can vary depending upon whom you hang with. Be selective of your friends and associates.

And perhaps even more important is to be aware of how your energy affects others. Sometimes it might feel like you are swimming against the current when you are in positive mode, but those around you are not. Your feelings and attitudes can affect all those around you, so be acutely aware of what type of energy you give off. And as life happens, we can only do the best that we can, depending where we are in our own lives.

In summary, if your life is working well for you, it may be because you are hanging with positive thinking people. If not, reconsider your associations.

Chapter 7
DNR
Do Not React

How often have we exploded in anger, destroyed or altered a relationship, or perhaps even lost a job? We might have been in the right and our anger justified, but still our reaction may have been destructive to our well-being.

This human condition has one biologically based behavior, and that is to react with full force whether we are threatened by a saber tooth tiger, an angry boss, or perhaps just an irritated mate. It is commonly called the fight-or-flight response. In our primitive biological evolution, to take time to think when threatened may have been fatal.

Knowing this, how can we act (not react) responsibly when threatened by either the mythical saber tooth tiger or more frequently by the numerous of potential conflicts that eventually will occur in our lives? There is an old adage that says, "Count to ten before reacting," and this often works to override our instinctual fight-or-flight reaction. Very often, however, this primitive instinct may take over, and our reaction may result in a personal disaster.

I do have a device that I have used in my own life and have at times suggested to clients. That is simply writing on my left wrist with the bold letters DNR, a visual reminder of Do Not React. An alternative, which I have found to be even more effective, is placing a thick rubber band on my wrist as a reminder. When approaching what I think might be a stressful encounter and I feel the emotional temperature rising, I glance at the DNR reminder on my wrist or snap the rubber band and often an emotional meltdown can be avoided.

And even as effective as these tools can be, they do require foresight just to look at the reminder or to snap the rubber band. Try them. They really work.

Chapter 8
Listening

Communication is such an important part of our lives that we hardly notice it. We speak, we text, we sing, we e-mail, we express with body language and with the tone of our voice, or we give a look. The list is endless.

Listening is perhaps the most important aspect of communication, yet it is also the most frequently overlooked.

When one truly listens, hears, and understands the other, dialogue is possible. And when there is true dialogue, real connection can be made.

Often in conversations, many of us can hardly wait for our turn to speak. This urgency to speak can totally occupy our minds, to the extent that we hardly listen to what the other is saying. At times this urgency will literally cause us to blurt out and cut the other person off. And often times this sends the message to the person that we are communicating with that we are not really interested in what he or she has to say.

I have known a few people who noticed that their relationships were not working for them. When they took the time to really look at themselves, they noticed that their communication skills were lacking because they were not authentically listening. As a result, they were not connecting in a meaningful fashion with people in their lives. So they decided to make a conscious choice (that I like to call *conscious resolve*) to be listeners. Their lives and relationships changed noticeably.

In my work with individuals, couples, and families, communication is the most frequent problem expressed. If your relationships are not working for you, consider if whether or not you are a good listener. Perhaps it's time to make your *conscious resolve*.

Chapter 9
The Talking Stick
An Exercise in Listening

There is a custom in Native American culture known to some as the tradition of The Talking Stick. It was used in powwows, which in Indian circles translates to a gathering of nations or a meeting. As the custom describes it, a single stick is passed around the circle and each person takes a turn to hold it. No one is allowed to speak until it is his or her turn to hold the stick.

This tool can be used effectively in any relationship. The key is to not abuse the ritual. The best way to participate in this listening ritual is to agree to the sacredness of this method of solving disputes. This agreement should be made when there is no heat between the individuals.

We all at times have a tendency to talk and not to listen. In a marriage or any relationship, listening and understanding the feelings behind the words is crucial. Ask yourself, "What is my partner feeling?" and then respond to the feelings and not to the words. Too often carelessly selected words do not represent the feelings beneath. Be willing to apologize and be willing to forgive. Often times, couples are more committed to being right rather than truly listening to their partner. To be right does not necessarily make for happiness.

Whoever initiates this exercise by feeling that the issue is worthy of this ceremony begins the ritual by picking up the stick (or whatever object is agreed upon). The other must listen without comment. When the first person is done speaking, he or she passes the stick to the other, at which time the second person speaks his or her position, and the first person must refrain from any comment. Keep in mind that it is best to limit yourselves to a maximum (as per the agreement) of two go-rounds, but let that be the last of it. Be careful to not fall into a *you said, I said* type of debate. Defending or blaming is a trap to be avoided. It is all about hearing and acknowledging each other's position. The individuals will have agreed in advance, that after a second go-round, both will return to their respective lives and ponder what the other has said. The goal here is to hear and truly empathize with the other.

Chapter 10
Choices
The Choice Is Yours

Perhaps, the most pervasive myth in our culture is that we possess few real choices. Often we believe that our life's circumstances are forced upon us and that we live at the whim of fate rather than in response to the choices we make.

It is important to dispel this myth of *choicelessness* and make lifestyle changes that can have the greatest positive impact on your health, longevity, and happiness.

Going beyond the obviously significant issues such as smoking, nutrition, exercise, or stress management, there are deeper issues and choices that might be dealt with. Some of these are how we deal with anger and sadness, how we relate to others, how we play and love, our capacity for forgiveness, our trust, our honesty, and our spiritual values.

Make the choice to be in control of your own life.

Chapter II
Don't Be Afraid

Don't be afraid to ...

1. **Smile and say hello to a stranger.**
   You will be delighted with the smile that comes back.

2. **Tell someone you love that you love him or her.**
   Sometimes words speak louder than actions.

3. **Play like a child.**
   We don't stop playing because we grow old. We grow old because we stop playing. (George Bernard Shaw, Biography)

4. **Compliment someone sincerely.**
   It could make his or her day, and yours.

5. **Share a loving feeling with someone close to you.**
   Life is temporary, and tomorrow may be too late.

6. **Lend a helping hand.**
   The reward will be yours.

7. **Give yourself a gift.**
   Why not? Aren't you entitled?

8. **Say you are sorry.**
   Don't let your ego get in your way.

9. **Do a kind act for no reason.**
   How you feel about yourself will be the reward.

10. **Goof around sometimes.**
    We can all be too busy being serious. Laughter is the best medicine.

Just try these things and see how your life will change.

Chapter 12
Self-Esteem
A Key to Mental Health

Self-esteem is one of the most crucial aspects of the human personality. A positive self-esteem is literally the immune system of our emotional lives. It helps us in overcoming many of life's challenges and problems.

The lack of self-esteem is perhaps the most common factor present in those suffering from long-term emotional problems. Recognizing the subtle forces of low self-esteem in oneself can be challenging. However, it's critical that we understand how the negative and limiting ideas we may have about ourselves can impede both our ability to heal past wounds and also to envision a new and better future.

The *not liking yourself* syndrome can often spawn a myriad of other symptoms, which can consistently undermine any attempt to improve your life.

All of the causes of how we get to this are too numerous to mention. However some of the more frequent causes include well-intentioned but flawed parenting, broken relationships, emotional or physical abuse in childhood, or verbal abuse from employers.

How we got to this place of low self-esteem is not as important as what we can do to change it. The first step on the road to healing is to simply ask ourselves, "Is my life working for me?"

Another important inquiry might be, "Do I stand up for myself when necessary?" Self-destructive comments are also a sign that low self-esteem might be affecting one's life. Have you ever found yourself saying things like, "I'm so stupid" or "I never get anything right"? These negative self-commentaries only serve to reinforce false and limiting ideas that we might have about ourselves.

Until a magical time machine is invented, we will not be able change the past, but we certainly can change our present and our future. It just takes a commitment to doing it. Decide to launch a campaign to discover all of the great things about you.

Building self-esteem in children is probably the most important thing that a parent can do. It will affect almost every aspect of that child for rest of his or her life. Parenting can be a challenging task, but reinforcing the good qualities of one's children almost from birth on is vital. And it can be done even while teaching appropriate boundaries of discipline. Always, always reinforce the good things that a child is or does. Do not destroy that child's future with constant put-downs.

Positive self-esteem is one of the most important elements in our own mental health. We can gradually transform our lives by staying on the lookout for ways to reinforce our positive attributes while being careful not to be too critical about those areas where we still need improvement. Always look for opportunities to reinforce positive feelings about yourself and others. In this way our vision of our potential and ourselves can be transformed, opening the door to a life of unlimited possibility.

The following is a progression of steps that can be used to reassert you to yourself.

1. Focus on the good things that you are, and not on the things that you are not.
2. Make a list of all of the things that you really like about yourself and celebrate your strengths.
3. Pay attention to the good things that others think about you ... on the job, friends, and so on.

4. Practice self-forgiveness for your mistakes. We are all human and we all make mistakes.
5. Change the way that you talk to yourself. Do not put yourself down.
6. Stop judging yourself by unreasonable standards.
7. Act as if you believe in yourself. It will become your reality.

Chapter 13
Accepting and Treasuring
A Path to Peace

Many years ago a book was written by Gail Sheehy entitled *Passages* in which she described the various stages of life, from childhood to old age.

Our life is a passage during which many events occur that can be unpleasant or even tragic and may totally disrupt our lives. Accepting these occurrences, in some fashion, and moving on is often very difficult, yet is essential if we are to live a happy and meaningful life.

Just a few examples of these types of losses are divorce, loss of a job, death of a loved one, major disappointments, and financial catastrophes. Health issues can be even more devastating. The effects of aging such as progressive physical impairment, decreased mental acuity, or diminished vision and hearing can be overwhelming.

As we travel this passage that we call life, for most of us happy and even delicious events do occur. Examples would be special friendships, walking on the beach with a loved one, a graduation, or the birth of a child. The list is endless, but what is important is to notice these joyful events when they occur, label them as *treasures* and preserve them in our memory as best and as vividly as possible. These treasures can be our best tools during the process of accepting.

Accepting and treasuring are both therapeutic and hopefully part of the same process. They can also be part of cultivating a sense of peace amidst the ever-changing realities of our life.

Without remembering the treasures, accepting can be a dismal and emotionally damaging event. Accepting alone can color one's perception of life in a negative fashion for years to come, resulting in a pessimistic outlook that has its own painful consequences.

When those damaging events do occur, (as they do in most of our lives) remember the treasures. Turn up the volume on these happy experiences of the past and replay them. If you can do this, even while dealing with and accepting a painful experience, it can help make emotional survival possible even during the most difficult of times. It takes practice, but with conscious effort, it can be done. In doing so, we become the creator of our own destiny, able to lead a life not colored by a sense of loss, but rather by a feeling of peace and a gratitude for the many treasures that we have experienced.

Chapter 14
The Time Machine

How often in our lives have we wished for a magical time machine that would allow us to go back and change our past. At first glance it sounds like an incredible idea. It would be wonderful if we could go back and change all of our *stuff* from the past, and literally come up in the present, clean as a whistle.

We often tend to focus on the things that we are not, rather than the things that we are. We are who we are today (the great qualities, and perhaps the not so great qualities) because of our past. We did not come from nothing.

We all operate our lives on what we believe to be our truths. These truths are products of everything that we have ever experienced. The purpose of our time machine travel is to examine and perhaps reinterpret some of these past events in the light of our present wisdom.

On our imaginary trip into the past, we might be able to put a different interpretation or twist on certain events. Such things as a parent who demeaned us, how we just could not get into the top social clique, or how the other kids made us feel ugly, and a thousand other events might be construed differently when reexamined with today's wisdom. Much of our original interpretation might have been the product of a blurred, hurt, or angry mind.

And yes, some of our traumas were real and perhaps cannot be reinterpreted in any beneficial way. However, it may not be necessary to spend years in psychoanalysis to arrive at the *aha* moments about our lives and the events that made us who we are today.

Most of us are stuck in the present (or the future) and seldom take time to critically reexamine the past events in our lives. In our imaginary journey, we might be able to reinterpret certain events and perhaps forgive others or ourselves for the most major to the most minor missteps along the way.

When you travel back and review the many possible interpretations of past events, one particular different reinterpretation may literally stand out and ring a bell and seem to strike home more than the others. This alternative interpretation is most likely not just a random thing, but may be coming from your unconscious and just might be a truth that you have missed.

In summary, if we view with an open mind the truths by which we operate, and keep our minds and hearts open, other possible interpretations may emerge for consideration and can change the reality by which we operate today.

The fact is, our time machine can have great value, but it does take determination and effort to get on board.

Chapter 15
The Connection

How often have you thought of someone to whom you have not spoken for years, and then he or she calls you in the very next few minutes? Or one day you meet a new person, and both of your lives change forever in what seems to be a most meaningful way. Perhaps you go into a room full of very depressed people, and you seem to *catch it* (the depressed mood that is). Many of us might remember when, as a child, our mother may have kissed an *owee* and the pain magically disappeared. How can this be possible? The approach of present day science described below may be the answer.

Modern physics has gone through many revelations in recent years ranging from the Unified Field Theory clear through the Superstring Theory and beyond. The bottom line of most of this research is that the basic building blocks of the universe seems to be energy, which according to the various theories may be configured in many forms. Our physical universe, the planets, the rocks, our bodies, our brains, and our thoughts, seem to be made up of the same stuff. Some postulate that the universe is one vast web of interconnecting energy waves.

So far no one theory has covered all of the corners, but unity and interconnectedness seem to be a common theme. The essence of the concept of *The Connection* is that everything is connected to everything.

Keeping this in mind, we may be able to make sense of those

seemingly remarkable coincidences that we all have experienced. But perhaps of greater importance is realizing that life is not a random occurrence, but in many ways we do have control over it. The *Power of Positive Thinking*, as described in the book by Norman Vincent Peale, is not a myth. You will become whatever your thoughts are. And YOU DO have control over your thoughts.

Experiences of many people seem to bear out this idea of interconnectedness. Groups or individuals may pray for an improved health outcome for another person, and the positive results have been statistically validated. It has been shown the health of optimists can often be far better then the health of pessimists. The process of guided imagery has often miraculously affected disease and also been known to affect the direction of one's life. Here the key seems to be *the energy of intention*. The possibilities are endless.

Look carefully at the thoughts that occupy your mind on a daily basis. If you do not like what you see, through self-discipline, you can change these thoughts and thereby change your life. It takes doing, but it can be done.

Chapter 16
Dealing with Mood Swings

Mood swings can be a normal part of one's life. One day we may feel on top of the world, and later in the same day we can feel lethargic and beaten down or overcome with anxiety. And these normal mood swings may be due to an endless number of causes, just some of which are the side effects of medication, hormone imbalance, birth control pills, caffeine, PMS, pregnancy, dehydration, and very often, the everyday stresses of one's life.

However, at times these mood swings can be so severe as to interfere with our functioning in our everyday life. Bipolar disorder is an example of this. In this condition we can cycle from being manic to being depressed to the point of being disabled. In cases such as this and other severe conditions, professional help should be sought.

And just what are some of the steps that one can take to deal with the relatively normal mood swings of one's life? Most often this is a funk or at other times a period of anxiety from which you are unable extract yourself. And if so, how can we change our lives to minimize the effects of these mood swings that have become unmanageable?

Certainly stress can be a major factor in mood swings. For one thing, you might step back and take a look at your life. Rethink the external pressures that are causing the stresses in your life and are your assumed consequences of certain events appropriate and reasonable. You may want to get the support of a friend to help in this determination. *Reperceiving* events in our lives in a positive or at least neutral framework can help to short circuit the process and minimize or even eliminate our stress response.

When you are doing your self-examination, consider if you are engaging in polarized thinking where you see things only in black or white, good or bad, or are you able to see the gray in between? Or are you over generalizing or focusing on one event as a predictor of disaster in your life?

One method proven to be effective is physical exercise, which may be very difficult to engage in when one is overcome with a down mood. But most often if you can push yourself to do it, the resulting endorphins can create miracles. And believe it or not, dehydration can be a factor, and drinking a sufficient amount of water daily can make a difference.

Doing a spring cleaning can work miracles. Clean your closet or your garage. The clutter of your life may be overwhelming you. The process of cleaning can in itself make you feel good about yourself. An aspect of this is just to stay busy. Get out, do errands, even go shopping. Take care of some of the details of your life that need taking care of.

Help someone. Here the time and effort involved in this process of helping another can help you to get outside of yourself. Also the sense of accomplishment is in itself fortifying.

There are no easy answers to the problem of dealing with the normal mood swings of life. The issue of mood swings can be quite burdensome, but if possible do take some positive action to overcome the swings to funks or periods of anxiety that can envelop any of us at difficult times in our lives.

Chapter 17
The Heartbeat
Skepticism, a Personal Story

I have come to be a believer in the unity of all things, and how at a personal level this belief validates my work in doing energy healing. But then every so often, for whatever reason, I seem to lose faith in the process. I become skeptical and almost a nonbeliever.

Then, seemingly not by accident, an event will occur in my life that is so obviously a manifestation of the whole process about which I had become skeptical, that I am put back on track. My belief system is restored and reinforced to an even higher degree. These events are so remarkable that I must either deny my senses that perceived them or accept them as the lesson that I need. The following event is one of those occurrences.

A young woman had sought my services on occasion for physical injuries that she had incurred as a gymnast. This time I had chosen to do absent healing over the phone. We had established our connection, which was quite palpable to both us. I asked how she was feeling, and she said that she felt a pronounced throbbing in her body.

This had never occurred when I worked with her in person or occasionally over the phone. When I asked her to describe the throbbing, she used her voice rhythmically to describe the rate of the throbbing. The rhythm was exactly that of my own heartbeat. We checked, and rechecked the rhythm, and there was no denying that our heartbeats had become accurately synced. Whether she was picking up my heartbeat, or I was picking up hers, it was an event that literally shook us both. The impact on both of us and her family was profound, and we will never forget it.

Certainly in my life this was a most remarkable event. But these incidents come in a variety of forms, ranging from a remarkable healing to how my thoughts may almost magically manifest a dream I had held. These lessons always seem to come when I need them most and always seem to help me regain direction in my life.

Chapter 18
Listen to Your Heart

The Western culture in which we live teaches us to use logic and reason as the most important factors in determining how we run our lives. But I have found that there is another equally or perhaps more important source of information and that is what I call our *heart*. This is often known by other names such as *gut feeling* or *intuitive sense*. I have often learned in retrospect that these feelings are valid more often than not.

A common example is in the area of romantic attachment. I have noticed when counseling someone coming out of a bad relationship that the individual may say something like, "I had a bad feeling about this from the start, but I did not honor it." But then, perhaps because of need or hormones, she or he went against this intuitive sense.

The fact is, in my experience, this alternative source of information may come from more than one's unconscious—it may also come from an even more interesting place, and that is where we connect with *all that is* or a combination of both. It is my belief that everything is connected. This gut feeling does not come from nowhere.

Practice listening to your heart. Give those feelings validity. Do not cast them aside. Let these feelings play a part in the decisions that you make in your life, and see how perhaps your life may change.

Chapter 19
Feelings Are

We have many options in our lives: where we live, our vocation and education, our spouse and our passions. The list is endless. One arena where the options are not so obvious is how does one feel. Feelings, whether joyful, sad, or in between, usually occur without our permission.

But if you are unhappy, sad, or just not at peace for any one of a thousand reasons, much of the time you are alone with your feelings. How often have you heard someone say, "Get over it" or similar words as you seem to stay stuck in a difficult place in your feelings? Perhaps you have suffered the loss of a loved one, and many months or even years have passed and a well-meaning friend might say something like, "It is time to move on." Usually, this does not help.

Grief is one of the most painful emotions, and it different for each person. Time does tend to heal, but at different rates for different people. Sometime the feelings of loss are never dissipated. The process cannot be rushed. When a genuinely caring person inquires as to how you are feeling and you are overwhelmed with feelings of sadness, I believe the healthy thing is to share your feelings. It really can help.

Feelings are based on emotions, and emotions often have their origin in the heart. But feelings can be affected by one's attitude. We have all experienced people with very positive attitudes and also people with negative attitudes. These are two very concrete and opposite ways that some people deal with life. What I am suggesting is that our attitudes are indeed optional. We do have choices, but at times the choice to change is not easy.

How we interpret certain events can be based on our attitude, and that can affect our feelings about that event. And for sure, life does happen, and sadness does occur. Our attitudes are more stable and less transient than the feelings that develop around a particular circumstance.

My thought is that if there is any way that a person can consciously change his or her attitude in a positive direction, the difficult feelings that of necessity arise in life will be much easier to handle and might even have a different flavor. This change would be about paying attention in every moment of the day to your language and thoughts. Keep it positive, and correct your thoughts as you go along. This *positivity* can become a habit.

I would not be so bold as to say that happiness is a goal in life, but I would venture to say that peace is. And peace is indeed a feeling. We all know what it feels like to not be at peace.

Feelings such as love and caring may be balanced off against feelings like fear and anger, but feelings will always be there. It is an essential part of the human condition. I would not want it to be otherwise.

Just remember, how you feel is how you feel, and that is the reality of it all.

Chapter 20
Go Fly a Kite
The Least Expensive Form of Therapy

People all ages are known to be passionate about kite flying. We often think of this just for children. Not true. I have seen fathers helping their small child fly a kite, and I have been flying kites for many years, and I am eighty-five. Besides the actual experience, you will meet a whole group of people the likes of whom you would have never met otherwise. And what can also be delightful is that a stranger may just come up and talk to you about your kite, especially if it beautiful.

It is truly an *experiential* experience. The most obvious thing is that you are out of doors in what is most often a beautiful environment. Perhaps the most wonderful thing about kite flying is that you are totally in touch with the wind, the sun, the trees around you, the sky, the clouds, and much more.

Watching where the wind comes from, and somehow helping your kite catch it just right as it soars into the sky, is a very special experience. And there is nothing like the tactile feeling of holding the line and playing the kite.

One of things that I find really exciting is holding the line up to my ear and actually hearing the sound of the wind on the string. I once did this for a small child who was watching me fly my kite, and the look on his face could best be described as *awestruck*.

The bad news is that this hobby can become addictive. The next hit may be the urge to purchase a larger, more expensive and even more beautiful kite. In my case that urge was satisfied by buying large stunt kite, which actually pulled me across the ground in a strong wind.

One might ask, what about this experience is therapeutic? All of the above can get you totally outside of yourself. You can be literally one with nature. You are only present in the moment. No need to wear a costume of something you are not. No need for Prozac or Xanax. You are just there: totally in the now. I recommend this as perhaps the least expensive form of therapy.

Chapter 21
Drowning in a Glass of Water

I recently had a challenge in my life where the outcome of my actions, at the very worst, would have been minimal and most likely would not have occurred at all. However, the thought of the possible negative consequences overwhelmed me and literally took over my life. I was doing one of the things that I do best, and that is *catastrophizing*. My wife, in an effort to help me see my dysfunction said, "Why are you drowning yourself in a glass of water?" Well put, I thought. What a perfect expression of what I seemed to be doing to myself.

Others might call it *awfulizing* or making a mountain out of a molehill, and there are many other terms for the same thing. And so how can one avoid drowning in a glass of water and still be reasonably cautious in one's life? I have found that it is very difficult to get outside of myself and look realistically at the actions or problems that I am facing unless I have some sort of a plan.

What I am suggesting is a tool, which we might call a *reality check box* of the issues that you are facing. This is a device that I have found useful in order to systematically evaluate the validity of my concerns.

The following are just a few of the thoughts that I suggest be placed into that box and considered. And there may be many more in any individual's case:

1. List the fears and concerns that may be consuming you.
2. How valid are the *what ifs* that seem to engulf you?
3. Understand that in life stuff happens. No one is exempt. How we deal with it is optional.
4. Realize that fear is a normal part of the human condition.
5. Know that our perceptions are colored by our life experiences, and these perceptions may not represent reality.
6. All of this is part of our natural survival instinct, be it a perceived physical danger or a perceived emotional or social consequence.
7. These considerations are not meant to negate events or actions that may be genuinely perilous.

And how does one use this tool? I suggest that you list your fears and concerns on paper and then go over these considerations listed as you honestly evaluate the likelihood of your fears being manifested.

Next I suggest attempting to get outside of yourself and view these perceived threats from a third person's viewpoint.

And finally, if need be, talk to a friend. The process of verbalizing and hearing yourself talk can often lead to clarity, as can suggestions from your friend.

I truly believe that this process can help prevent one from drowning in a glass of water much of the time. With my wife's help, in my case, it did.

Chapter 22
The Fitted Sheet
Our Need to Feel Secure

A fitted sheet is a special bed sheet that fits over a mattress in such a fashion that the four corners of the sheet fit over and around the four corners of the mattress. Most of us at some time or other have used a fitted sheet. When it is new, it always fits perfectly. Then we wash it, it shrinks, and it will no longer cover all four corners unless we lift up the fourth corner or in some other fashion we wrestle it on.

This can be a metaphor for life. In our lives we want to know that *all of the corners are covered*. We want to feel secure. It's just about impossible to cover all of the corners of life, no matter how hard we try. We buy car insurance, house insurance, health insurance, life insurance, any other kind of insurance to cover almost every possible negative *perhaps* of human life. The struggle for this need to feel secure can also take other forms, such as religion, the need for money in the bank, power, possessions, burglar alarms, relationships, and so much more.

There seems to be a biological basis for this human condition to feel secure. It is very real, and appears not to be optional. This is best demonstrated in the early stages of life when a child attaches to a caregiver who the child believes will keep him or her safe. We often carry this need for attachment into our adult life when we find a friend or a partner who makes us feel secure and safe. I remember as a child *knowing* that my parents could and would always take care of me. I also remember that as I began to mature, I realized that this belief was not necessarily true.

Although the need to feel secure (literally to *cover all of the corners*) is a natural principal, it can operate as a destructive force in our life if we are unaware of its workings. If our preoccupation with the need to feel secure grows into a state of constant fear, it can seriously disrupt our ability to function easily in relationships and can change the course of our life. There are many ways that this can express itself. Some examples are self-sabotage, inappropriate partner selection, defective financial planning, bad choices of chosen profession, and many other maladaptive behaviors.

This aspect of the human condition of needing to feel secure may be tough to accept. There are no easy answers, but here are a few suggestions:

1. Be aware that this fact of life is important. This awareness can be an emotional buffer when less-than-great things do occur.
2. Work hard to develop and maintain a positive attitude. This alone can actually alter the events of life in a positive way.
3. Take time to communicate your fears and concerns in a calm and empowering way to people in your life when it is appropriate. Work on clarity and understanding as an antidote to paranoia or suspicion.
4. Take care of your body as best you can in order to avert any untoward health crises.
5. Be very conscious about keeping your finances in order to avoid insecure feelings.
6. Be aware of the biology of the need to feel secure, and be extremely wary of any unhealthy relationships into which you might be drawn. Learn to enjoy time alone and trust your intuition about others.

Chapter 23
The Big T in Marriage
And Relationships

There is an old song that some may remember called "Love and Marriage" written by Sammy Cahn and Jimmy Van. There is an equally important song that might be written called "Trust and Marriage."

Trust is one of the most fundamental requirements in successful and lasting human relationships. It is closely connected to the need to feel secure. One might say that the level of Trust between two people is the thermometer of the quality of that partnership.

One of the most important aspects of Trust is that it needs to be a mutual condition shared by both parties. It is about always believing in your partner and knowing that you are always going to be believed in by your partner.

Trust of one's partner can also be a vital aspect of building self-esteem.

It allows us to move past the fear that often keeps us separate from each other. As that separation and fear dissolve, we are more and more able to see each other through the eyes of love and acceptance. What a gift it would be for our partner to pay attention to all good things we are, rather than the things that we are not. And what a gift to be able to offer our partner the same.

Trust can progressively be built as we shed our protective shells and expose who we really are to our partner. Only when we can share our dreams, our fears, our secrets, our uniqueness, and sometimes our not such great qualities and know that we will still be accepted is Trust established. It is about the awareness that there is no need to wear a costume of who we are not. Only when we know that we can be open and honest can real Trust be established.

When Trust is present, it may or may not be a spontaneous occurrence. It can be a process that can extend over time and may require real work and commitment on the part of both partners. There may be times when the partners back off or grow closer during the process.

When we receive this gift of Trust from our partner and are validated for who we really are, it becomes easier for us to experience our own innate value. For many of us, this has a huge impact on our ability to be a positive force in our own relationship and in the world.

Caution: when honesty is not allowed, anger and resentment can occur. Beware of the signs.

Chapter 24

A Prayer Is Answered

Over the many years, I have studied and taught about the interconnectedness of all things and how prayer may be a part of that. And every so often the universe delivers me a lesson on this subject, often when I need the lesson the most. This might be in the form of a miracle or an answer to a prayer. The following is a description of one such event in my life.

Twenty-six years ago I was feverishly studying for the orals part of my licensing exam to become a therapist. This is a particularly difficult exam where it is known that there is usually only a 33 percent pass rate with a 67 percent failure rate. A good friend of mine was praying that I would pass that very difficult exam. The night before the exam I resolved that I would not open one more book in an effort to anticipate any one of the thousands of questions that might be thrown at me. But I couldn't resist a subtle feeling that I should open a particular book just one more time. I read only the first paragraph that I laid my eyes on, one that was on a very fine point of law that dealt with psychotherapists. The next day the examiners asked me a question that dealt specifically with the very point of law that I studied the night before. I knew that fine point so well that I even pretended to stumble in recalling the answer.

Was it a coincidence that I had opened to the exact passage I would need to know that day? Or was it something much more? In my heart I clearly sensed that the prayer and intention of the one who held me in their thought had produced what seemed to be a real miracle.

Other such miracles, or lessons, are described elsewhere in this book. These lessons seem to always occur when I needed them the most.

Chapter 25
Expectations: Lessons to Be Learned

The word *expectation* sounds like a fairly benign word, and at times it has the potential for creating great joy. But at other times it can be a source of great difficulty and disillusionment and can become a force that can rule us in a most destructible fashion.

The most significant expectations are

1. expectations that we have of others;
2. expectations that we have of ourselves; and
3. expectations that others have of us.

Perhaps the most painful area is where we place expectations on others. This can set us up for major disappointments. An example would be when our children or other loved ones forget a special occasion (like birthdays or Mother's Day) or in the workplace when we work so terribly hard and no anticipated recognition is ever forthcoming.

The second mentioned area can be the unreasonable expectations that we place on ourselves. This could have had its origins in unconscious input from our childhood, our culture, or any of a multitude of other aspects of our lives (of which we are unaware). An example would be the need to always be perfect. The difficulty with this type of compulsion is that the sources of it may be unconscious and very difficult to access. This can involve real soul searching or perhaps even therapy.

The third area, perhaps the most subtle and potentially damaging to the psyche, is when we work to fulfill the expectations of others and when, in doing so, we are not being honest with what we truly want to do or be. The hazard is that the more that we give ourselves away to please others, the more difficult it may be to retrieve who we really are.

Whether you are expecting things of others or of yourself, or others are expecting of you, it can and should be an optional process. Other terms or ways of thinking that we might use in place of expectation could be *hope* or *desired outcome*. Expectation, on the other hand, is an all-or-nothing concept and leaves no room for alternatives.

For those who have the ability, just letting go of expectations in any form is the method of choice. This means really knowing who you are, and that who you are is truly okay. Another way to look at it is that others who might expect of you have the problem, not you. Literally, you are in charge of you.

Another aspect of the expectation process is to stop and talk to yourself. Ask yourself, if such and such does or does not happen, have I set myself up for pain or disapproval? If the answer is yes, can I handle the outcome? Depending on the answer, it may be important to go through a change of thought process whereby other outcomes become acceptable.

Chapter 26
Stuffing It
Or Better, Just Say No

O ne evening I was driving with a friend of mine when my friend made a fairly innocuous remark, which under normal circumstances shouldn't have bothered me in the least. Instead, I flew into a rage and jammed my hand through the windshield of my car. Total cost of the event was $400 for the windshield and years of therapy costing several thousand dollars.

In my particular case, this disorder might be termed the *stuff it now, and explode later* syndrome. This syndrome is very common in a group of people that I have chosen to call *people pleasers*. I did identify myself as member of this group.

What I perceive in the personality of these people is that there literally seems to be a place somewhere in body or psyche where we literally stuff all of the things that we have done or said to please others. And this place has a limited capacity and is *nonelastic*. Then on that particular day when I attempted to stuff just one more thing into this *nonelastic* container, I exploded and destroyed the windshield of my precious 280Z car.

Yes, it is true, most of us truly like to be liked, and this need is usually socially acceptable. But when this need becomes maladaptive for ourselves, then one must take stock and see why life is perhaps not working as well as it might.

One aspect of being a people pleaser it is that is that it hard say NO. They often cannot express their real feelings, they avoid showing their real anger, and they find it easier to be nice than not. The common trait is that they tend to give themselves away in favor of others.

The ability to say NO appropriately is most important. And sometimes these people are so used to pleasing that it may be difficult for them to determine what they truly want to do. Sometimes one has to consciously look deep inside oneself and determine what he or she really, really wants, because people pleasing can become a pathological process.

I have a theory about life in general, and being a pleaser in particular. I believe that most of us want to be liked. This is part of the fabric of our society. The issue here is about to what self-damaging extremes some of us will go to satisfy that need.

This can be a subtle process, and it can literally sneak up on you. If life seems not to be working for you, and those around you seem genuinely happy, then take a look inside yourself. Make sure that the people pleasing process is not robbing you of your voice, your self-determination, and your authenticity.

Chapter 27
Stress: The Silent Killer

Much has been said about stress and the deleterious effect that it can have on our lives. However, I have never heard of it being on a death certificate as the cause of death. Unfortunately, it is all too frequently a contributory cause to many diseases or even death.

Most of us know that acute stress historically has served a very useful purpose in lives of human beings. In our early beginnings, when the tiger or the enemy attacked us, a complex system of hormones was set into motion and the *fight-or-flight* reaction that resulted was our adaptation for survival. Just some of the physiological responses to this emergency stimulus are an increase in blood pressure, elevated blood sugar levels, a suppression of the immune system, and much more. But when the stimulus of this kind of stress dissipates, so does the fight-or-flight response. Things return to normal in a very short time.

However, in our society today, chronic stress is the demon. Just some examples of causes of chronic stress would be frustration on the job, loss of control in one's life, a bad marriage, fear of financial loss, and more. Unfortunately, this type of stress does not just go away. It can become the physiological costume that we wear most of the time. Just a few of the many manifestations that we might see today could be heart problems, gastric ulcers, headache, abdominal pain, hypertension, irritable bowel syndrome, and cancer. Certainly there are many other factors involved in these illnesses, but chronic stress is at the very least a frequent and all too often a contributing factor.

It is well known in medical circles that one's health and longevity can be greatly improved by reducing chronic stress. The good news is that most of the time we can have control over this aspect of lives. It's just about making certain lifestyle choices, physically and psychologically, and then sticking to them. I have witnessed people who happened to have survived a first heart attack, and as the result, they completely turned around their lifestyle. Why wait what for something like this to happen? See the following ten choices that you can make to reduce stress.

Chapter 28
Ten Choices You Can Make to Reduce Stress

1. Say no! The test is, "Will anybody die if I don't do _____?" Then make a choice based on what you truly desire to do.
2. Avoid perfection. Beware of the disease of being *overly perfectionistic*. Relax your standards.
3. Focus on understanding, rather then being understood. Focus on loving, rather than on being loved.
4. Play hard and often. Make it a nonnegotiable part of your life.
5. Take one day at time. Now, today, is the only time that we really have. Try not to destroy it by worrying about the past or the future.
6. Exercise regularly. If you can include it as part of play, all the better.
7. Use *Pollyanna Powder*. Count your blessings when life becomes difficult.
8. Accept that you cannot cover all the bases in life. Learn to live as comfortably as possible with the uncertainties of just being.
9. Establish contingency plans. Put spare money in the checking account, hide extra keys, allow extra time, fill the gas tank, make repairs when needed, and so on. Be your own insurance company.
10. Be as authentic as you can be. The load is lighter when you are who you are.

Chapter 29
The Hot Stove and Red Flags
On Relationships

Have you ever touched a hot stove? For those of us who have, we would not dare touch a hot stove a second time. Even the smallest child learns that early on. Then why is it (at an emotional level) that many of us as adults do not learn from our past experiences, as the child does?

In dealing with relationships, the red flag usually shows up as that vague, negative feeling, far down inside, that says, "Seems like I have been here before." Each relationship wears a different costume. And because of this different costume, we truly believe that this time it will be different. Oftentimes, only in retrospect, do we notice our repetitive and perhaps maladaptive behaviors.

We all have an intuitive sense. Most of the time we can really *read* that other person, but perhaps for of whatever reason, we may not listen to that intuitive glimmer.

There is another piece of the picture. The red flags may go up, but we do not heed them because we believe that we can change the other person. Most of us do not change very easily. And ask yourself, in this relationship, how much can I really change? At least you are in control of you, but most often you are not in control of the other.

So what to do? Do not touch that hot stove again. Do pay attention to your gut feelings. There is usually good information there. And usually now is better than later.

Chapter 30
How Does Energy Healing Work?

Healing has been around for many thousands of years and has existed in almost all cultures. The medicine man of our Native American Indians is just one example. Many primitive cultures attribute the healings to their Gods, or spirits, or other entities. And perhaps these notions are not so far from the truth when they are viewed in the context of the culture in which they originate.

One of the more recent concepts in the area of healing is called *bioenergy*. To put this in more concrete terms, it is thought by many that energy fields are a part of all biological systems. It is believed that perhaps these fields permeate and extend beyond these biological systems. It is also believed by some that they may connect in some fashion with all things at all levels. Essentially this description sounds much like the concept of *unity*.

There are no conventional scientific theories that explain spiritual or energy healing. Here are a few of the concepts and ideas, proposed within the spectrum of complementary/alternative medicine (CAM), or bioenergy medicine:

1. The bioenergies of a healer can produce positive changes in the energy fields of those desiring healing.
2. The intentions, a healer can produce positive changes in the energy fields of those desiring healing.
3. The intentions of a healer can produce positive changes in

      the awareness of those desiring healing and thereby affecting any physical or psychological problems that need healing.

4.   Somehow in energy healing there seems to be a process by which only those areas that require healing are affected.

5.   The concept that healing is not restricted in time or space is described by such terms as: Universal Mind, Cosmic Consciousness, Nonlocal mind, or One Mind. This describes how perhaps our consciousness can reach out and connect with others, even at great distances. This idea gives an understanding of how absent or distant healing might occur.

In distant or absent healing, the healer may be many miles from the person that the healer is intending to heal. Somehow a connection is made. The results of this form of healing have been validated by double blind studies. Prayer can be classified as this form of healing.

Some healers are able to see a person's aura and also sense the energy of their chakras, which may give the healer information about the physical and psychological condition of the person seeking healing.

The important key seems to be the intention of the healer. This can operate in the presence of the client or also when doing absent healing. The healer may place his or her hand on or just above the affected area. It seems that this may be one way of focusing his or her intention on the area to be treated. Also the energy and intent of the healer can be transmitted by merely holding his or her hands over the hands of the individual desiring healing.

There are a broad range of healing therapies that view the psychological state and the body as a single unit, sometimes referring to this as the *mind-body*. When this is put in a spiritual context, it is often referred to as the *mind-body spirit*. Some of the healing therapies embrace this concept are: massage, reflexology, applied kinesiology, healing touch, therapeutic touch, Reiki healing, energy healing, and many more.

Often it is asked if one needs to have faith in the process. There is no research evidence to suggest that faith is required for healing. Animals, plants, and other organisms have responded to healing energy. However, studies have shown that believing in your body's ability to heal itself and having that faith, can certainly speed the healing process up significantly.

Chapter 31
Fire and Wisdom

I believe that *fire* and *wisdom* are essential aspects of the human condition. Fire, as used here, is that drive that pushes us to accomplish and achieve. It is about *I Shall* or *I Will*.

Wisdom is a progressive and cumulative learning occurrence based on experience. It is the comprehension of what is true or right coupled with optimum judgment as to action. And there are no shortcuts.

In the book *Passages* written by Gale Sheehy, she described the various stages of life, which most of us do not notice as we progress through them. What I would like to address here are the various levels at which this fire burns over the course of our lives and how this fire relates to the gradual acquiring of wisdom. As I see it, there are three stages.

Stage one, which some of us may remember at a much younger age, might have been when we believed we could conquer the world and knew everything. I do remember profound errors that I made as a youth when I did not honor the wisdom of my very wise father. An example, in my case, was when two friends and I, at the age of nineteen, set out on a project to build a wooden sailboat and sail around the world. Common sense would have dictated otherwise, since we had no money or means to do it. The project failed. Lots of fire, but little wisdom.

In stage two, the good news is that there is a period of our lives when these two stages of fire and wisdom do overlap. The fire burns brightly as wisdom is gradually obtained. This I might call the time for optimum and effective action in one's life. The *I shall* quality of fire is now coupled with wisdom.

Also in this stage, others may have fire and wisdom combined just to find peace in their lives, with an occupation that would allow for that. And it may not apply to just a vocation. Other examples might be motherhood, studying economics, striving to become an Olympic champion, devotion to family, or entering the ministry. The list is endless.

And then in stage three, as the years pass, many of us may have progressively had our fire dimmed, but in its place we may have, hopefully, acquired more of that quality known as wisdom. And then we might ask ourselves, "Why did it take so long to get smart?" We are products of our experiences, and only time can produce this quality.

Stage three is where I seem to be today. Friends have suggested that I write a book that expresses the essence of the many articles that I have written. However my fire has dimmed and my thoughts are, "Well, maybe I will get around to it someday." Lots of wisdom, and still a little fire.

So what is the lesson here? Do have a dream and be aware of the changes of fire and wisdom in your life. If you have an idea, *do it now*. Do not put it off until *someday*. Today, when your fire burns brightest and wisdom is present, your *someday* should perhaps be today.

Chapter 32
Wish I Hadda ...
Living Life with the Fewest Regrets

Many times over the years we may have had an idea or an opportunity to do something that we really felt called to do. Sometimes this idea almost screamed at us. And this could have been in many areas of our life such as pursuing a certain profession, following a romance, going on a journey, buying a house, starting a business, or having children. The list of *perhapses* is endless.

And then, perhaps unfortunately, we may have let it slide and our thinking became something like, "Well, maybe next week, or next year." And then the opportunity to do it is gone. Years might go by, and then we may go through a process that I call *Wish I Hadda* ... Written fully it would read, "I wish that I would have done this or that." In case you haven't noticed, this thing called life flies by at an increasingly rapid pace. I believe that the more meaningful experiences that we put into our life, the more meaningful our life will be.

This does not mean that one should do just anything at the slightest whim. We must use reasonable judgment, and finances are often a factor. The idea is that many years later, when following that urge is no longer an option, we may regret not having done it or not even having tried, and then the dream becomes a *Wish I Hadda* ...

As I look back at my life, I have made many choices. Some were real winners, and unfortunately, others were not. But if I had not chosen to do some of the things that had not worked out, today I believe that I would have regretted not even making the attempt and they would have joined the list of *Wish I Hadda* ...

Give credibility to these urges and attempt to do as many of these worthwhile things as are achievable, so that as the years pass, the list of *Wish I Hadda* ... is as short as possible.

And finally, if one has a dream, it may happen. If there is no dream, it can never happen.

Chapter 33
Emotions and Pain
The Broken Heart

O ur emotions are certainly part of the human condition. The pleasant feelings imparted by these emotions can certainly add loveliness to our lives. However these emotions can also impart great pain: Not just emotional pain, but at times intense and real physical pain, such as chest pain, headache, stomach ache, back pain, and more.

How many of us have suffered an emotional trauma and found that a real pain seemed to occur somewhere in the body. This could be the breakup with a loved one, where the heartbreak can feel like our physical heart is really broken, or feeling crushed by a friend's harsh words. Innumerable other emotional assaults may come upon us: losing a job, a divorce, suffering an injury, lack of money, or the death of a loved one. Any of these may cause a real physical pain in our body and at times even physical illness.

Much research has been done on this subject, and the emotional pain that one feels is real and not psychological. Neurological research has indicated that there is shared brain circuitry, or put differently, there is one nerve pathway for pain, whether the cause is truly physical or emotional. The circuitry is the same. It has been shown that the areas of the brain that are involved in pain make no distinction between physical or emotional pain. This concept makes a clear case for the connection of the mind and body. It also explains why emotional distress can make us physically ill, and kindness can help sustain health.

It has been shown that the hormonal response in emotional trauma is very much the same as in physical trauma. Immediately after a physical injury, the body can become numb to pain for a brief period as the fight-or-flight reaction sets in. Likewise after an emotional or social assault, the individual may become numb to additional emotional or social assaults for a brief period.

Another important area to be considered is that when one is in physical pain, one can become emotionally depressed. A feeling of helplessness can ensue. Consider when one is fighting a serious illness, or suffering from the treatment of a serious illness, depression is often a consequence. At times when a cancer patient is receiving the various appropriate treatments, the adverse reactions of these treatments may so painful and devastating it can certainly cause an emotional state of hopelessness and depression. Pain and emotions are intertwined, and work in both directions.

There is a close association between chronic neuropathic pain conditions such as fibromyalgia and depression/anxiety. These are two distinct conditions, but perhaps by their shared circuitry they are often linked. It has been shown that those suffering from fibromyalgia may at times be helped by psychotherapy, which addresses the patients' psychological problems. This is not to say that pain of that disorder is not real.

Another important issue not to be overlooked is that at times, the medical community may be skeptical of the linkage of emotional to physical pain. When a physician's attitude is dismissive of inexplicable pain, a patient may feel more isolated and rejected. It is important that any medical approach is holistic and be in concert with the concept of the unity of the mind and body.

Chapter 34
Brief Karma

There is an expression I often hear, and that is, "What goes around, comes around." It sounds like a corny expression, and I have necessarily gone along with it. But a recent event validated this concept in my mind.

I was recently bike riding with a good friend of mine, and an apparently confused driver was weaving slowly through the area in which we were riding, making no signals or indications of what her intent was. My friend felt threaten by the driver and shouted at her both in fear and anger. A few minutes later, we had just finished grocery shopping at a market. My friend was pushing her shopping cart toward our car when someone driving a car shouted at her in anger, as if my friend did not know what she was doing.

Almost instantly my friend got the message. She was on the receiving end of what she had just dished out. The message was loud and clear. And brief karma was almost instant.

Chapter 35
How I Came to Be

I have been a registered pharmacist for fifty-five years, and have always been very scientifically oriented. About thirty-five years ago a remarkable event occurred that changed my life and ultimately brought me into your home today.

I had attended one of the many mind science workshops, which were common at that time. This class presented me with a whole new way of thinking. To put it simply, the idea was presented that everything is energy, everything is connected to everything, and with our thoughts we can affect and change our world.

On the last day of the class, the facilitator said something like, "We now will teach you to stop pain and bleeding by touching." My first thoughts were, "Yeah, right, that's a bunch of nonsense." But I did listen carefully to everything he said. Some weeks later, a friend of mine was experiencing a rather disabling shoulder pain, and she suggested that I use what I had learned to relieve her pain. I gave it a try, and much to our surprise, the pain vanished. And so on that day, armed with a new faith in what is possible, I began my journey.

I began by studying at The Healing Light Center in Glendale, California and eventually enrolled in their professional healer program. There I learned that through the power of thought and touch, it was possible affect the course of illness in others or ourselves.

Upon graduation, I began to practice energy healing, which at times proved amazingly effective. But I also discovered that much of the physical illness that I encountered may have had its roots in people's psychological and/or spiritual well-being or lack thereof. The energy healing might be effective only temporarily if people did not change their way of life.

I felt that I needed the additional tool of psychotherapy. In order to round out my education, I enrolled in the graduate psychology program at Antioch University in Los Angeles, California in order to become a psychotherapist. I now felt that I was much better trained to address the *whole person* on both a psychological and energy level. This method is commonly called *holistic*, and it is often referred to as a mind/body/spirit approach.

As I look back from where I started as pharmacist in 1957, it certainly has been a long and fascinating journey. And this is how I came to be who I am today, one who works professionally as a psychotherapist and who also practices energy healing.

I think that the lesson here might be to be open for anything. You never know what incredible gifts the universe might throw your way.

Chapter 36
The Power of Intention
A True Story by David Harris

I wonder how many of us comprehend the power of the words, "I can't." I believe that these words or thoughts may have doomed endless projects or dreams that might have otherwise been realized.

The opposite and much more effective approach is the power of the words "I shall," "I will," or "I can," which are so much more valuable in a positive direction and is what here I refer to as *The Power of Intention*.

Sometime in the period of 1975 to 1980, many Power of the Mind courses were being offered. Silva Mind Control was one, and Mind Psi-Biotics was another, and there many others. Some friends had told of the remarkable things could be done by one's thoughts, as taught in these classes. Out of idle curiosity, I did take one such weeklong course.

One of the many things that were taught was the power of imagery during a meditation. I did not really believe this alternative method could be effective in changing my life, but I decided to give it try. I had been a practicing pharmacist my whole life, and at the time of the class I was managing a medical pharmacy. This particular pharmacy had just come on the market, and I was contemplating buying it and doing what I had been trained to do my whole professional life.

However a very good friend of mine asked me, "But why do

you want to buy this pharmacy?" To which I replied, "Well, this is what I do." Her response was, "If that is the only reason, why don't think of perhaps other ways to create your ideal life?" Finally my friend convinced me to use the tools taught in course that I had just completed. She suggested that I put down on a paper all of the things that I want in my life, and let God fill in the *how* I would achieve these goals. I did just that. I wrote down and illustrated many of the things that I wanted for my family and myself and literally left it up to whatever power might manifest my dreams. I did a guided imagery as part of my daily meditation. I did this for about four months, and then unbelievably interesting things began to happen.

Roller-skating was the rage in Southern California, especially at the beaches. My daughter, Julie, then age thirteen, wanted a pair of roller skates, so we went together to the beach, where there were many skate shops to purchase a pair for her. I also purchased a pair for myself. Julie and I skated all over the San Fernando Valley. Then I began to wonder, there were so many thriving skate shops at the beach, why not one in the Valley? I ran the idea by several of my friends, and everyone said it would not work. Much too hot in the Valley, so my well-meaning friends said.

But something urged me to continue to pursue this goal. Many people were skating at Balboa Park in Van Nuys, California. Something near the park would be a perfect location. I remember one rainy day I was looking for a possible location across from the park. There were none. Then on a quirk, I walked into a box shop across from the park and asked the proprietor if he knew of a location. He said was moving at the end of the month, and that I should talk to the landlord about taking over this particular location. I did that, and asked for a one-year lease. Next day I returned for an answer, and the landlord offered a one-year lease, with a one-year option. This would be a deal totally in my favor.

I gathered every cent that I could muster and plunged forward to build and open the only skate shop in the Valley at that time. What was interesting was that I wasn't even nervous, even though I had put all they money that I had into this project. I was thinking only positively, and not a negative thought entered my head. I took over the location and remodeled the whole thing into a very flashy skate shop. On opening day, within two hours we had rented every one of the 175 skates that I had for rent, and sold many more besides. The shop was a smashing success. My shop and I were even featured on television. Everything worked, as if almost by magic.

I continued working for a short time in the pharmacy that I had thought of buying. But this roller skate business was really fun, and I was making a good living and enjoying every minute of it. Three months after we opened, my manager said that we urgently needed more space. Would you believe that the next day, the beauty shop that was adjacent to us said that we could take over their lease, which we did, and tripled our space and our business volume. I now became the full time proprietor my new creation. Indeed miracles were happening.

I had not really noticed until then, but every single thing that I had written down on my imagery sheet had occurred, and I had literally let God fill in the *how* it would all happen. I was making an excellent living. My entire family was working with me in the shop (as well as another six or seven employees). I looked forward to going to work every day. I had time to be with my family. I was now studying to become a healer, which was one of my goals, and eventually I began to teach classes in miracles, healing, and the power of thought and intention. As I looked over what I had created, it was truly a miracle, and the last thing that I ever would have predicted.

We ran the shop for three years, and as the skating craze faded, my lease expired, and I closed the shop with perfect timing.

So what is the message here? This event was the beginning of my voyage of discovery into the interconnectedness of all things. I learned that my thoughts can influence my life in a very real and positive way. Conversely, negative thoughts can also influence one's life in a very negative way. Also I learned that one's intentions can

David Harris

become a form of energy that assists oneself or others in healing. And I believe that all of this might be considered synonymous with prayer, which I have learned has tremendous power. Bottom line, all of this has convinced me that there is an intelligent force that is in charge of all things.

Chapter 37
Manifesting One's Dream

There are endless number of ways by which one might manifest one's dreams or aspirations by using the power of intention. There is no correct way, only your way. The following are steps that I have used.

1. Have a dream or goal, and believe that it is possible.
2. Write about and/or draw a picture of your dream. An example is that I have a sign on the wall over my desk, "Will ride bike for many more years." Or as in the previous chapter, I outlined my rather complicated goals in clear written detail and drawings.
3. Go into a meditative or relaxed state and visualize your dream or aspiration daily. Use all of your senses in your imagery: sight, sound, smell, touch, and emotional tone.
4. Do not sit down in a rocking chair in your living room waiting for it to happen, but get out into world and watch for signs that the universe has heard you.
5. Watch your world expectantly for opportunities that will be presented. Do not waste your effort on locked doors but move on to doors that might be opened.
6. Continue your guided imagery, and imagine what it will be like for you when your dream is realized.

I have used this tool of intention in virtually every aspect of my life from self-healing and healing of others to success in business.

Chapter 38
I Thought I Was Invincible

Life's lessons come to us in various forms over the length of our lives. These lessons, I believe, are our primary source of wisdom.

In my own life, I was quite literally an overachiever and felt that my mind and my body could handle anything. I truly thought I was invincible. Stress was literally my way of life.

And then in May 1993, my life changed forever. On the day that I was attending my son's graduation from medical school, the biggest lesson of my life struck. My speech began to falter. My thinking became confused. My son rushed me from his graduation celebration to the hospital in which he had been training.

I was suffering a stroke, and the disabilities were progressively becoming more severe. I remember during the admissions process, my right hand and lower arm would not respond and my thoughts came out jumbled when I attempted to speak. It was determined that surgery would have to be performed to prevent further clots from reaching my brain. But it then became apparent that during that surgery more clots were released and my disabilities became more pronounced. Now the whole right side of my body was affected. I had both physical and cognitive impairments. I could not remember how to use a knife and fork. I could not dial a phone. I had lost many of the ordinary skills by which we run our lives. After ten days in the hospital I was released to the care of a neurologist to rebuild my life.

For the next several months I was unable to drive or go to work.

I took a bus to get around. A totally different way of life became a necessity. My motor abilities gradually returned, but cognitive faculties were much slower to recover. Just being able to think remained quite difficult. It was frightening to wonder if I would ever be my old self again.

For many years I have taught people how a positive attitude and having an intention to overcome physical illness is very effective. I have never really had a need to apply it in my own life. Now I was being tested. I began to apply all of the tools that I had taught for so many years. These tools were based in the premise that there is a higher power, and we can tap into that power through many means, some of which are imagery, intention, or prayer.

The good news is that I did recover. I realized how lucky I was that I had virtually no obvious physical defects. But my life had been permanently impacted.

In retrospect, I looked at all of the factors that led up to that event. In fact I was doing my usual overachiever invincible thing. I was pushing my physical and mental body to the limits. I was working as a pharmacist, had a practice as a therapist, and opened a new business. I was working ninety plus hours a week. The stress level was extreme. My then-adult children cautioned me with words like, "Dad, stop it. You cannot handle all of this." My response was "Don't worry. I'm all right. I can handle it."

Well, obviously I did not handle it. And for sure I finally did learn my lesson, and that was that I was truly not invincible. Life's lessons were handed to me with a vengeance. And certainly my life did change.

Perhaps the most important lesson was that it was time to reevaluate what really matters in my life. I came to realize there were two things that mattered most. The first was that my family, and the time that I spent with them, was by far the most important thing. And the other was that *now* is truly the only time that we have, and we must make the most of it.

Chapter 39
Look for the Good Stuff

There is a human condition called *the human condition*. This may sound contradictory, but what I am referring to is that we all have our qualities, some of which may be interpreted by others as great, but at other times as not so great. The not-so-great qualities are often judged and referred to by others as *our stuff*.

We are all products of whatever we have gone through in our lives to this point. These formative events may be good or bad parenting, successes, failures, heartbreaks, being loved, or disappointments. The list is endless. We did not just happen to be who we are by accident.

It is so easy when evaluating those in our lives to notice and focus someone's not-so-great stuff and let it overshadow the rest of that person's really great stuff. In our habit of judging, we may miss the very essence of a wonderful person.

I know some individuals who by their very nature have the gift of seeing the best in everyone that they meet. They might be called *positive focusers*. And, how I see them in their lives is that they are extremely happy because of this quality.

We all have the option of being *positive focusers*. It is a wonderful gift that can be developed. But always remember, we, every one of us, do have our stuff.

Chapter 40
Miracles: A Dialogue with the Universe

At some time in our lives, an occurrence bordering on the miraculous may occur. I believe that these events are not random but actually brought into our lives as lessons to be heeded.

Definition of a miracle, per *Encarta Dictionary*: an event that appears to be contrary to the laws of nature and is regarded as an act of God.

To many, simple belief and acceptance of miracles is enough. To these lucky ones, a miracle is really not a miracle. It is rather the unfolding of the divine plan. It is just the way that things ought to be. A miraculous healing may not be a miracle at all; it is just expected. The religions of the modern Western world satisfy the needs of millions for the explanation of the phenomenon of miracles. To these people, prayers to an omnipotent being may be answered and their framework of reality is not shaken.

To others, faith and trust is not such an easy task. These people can only relate to what is scientific, rational, or provable. One of the several rational theories of miracles that can be alluded to is quantum physics in which the universe appears to be a dynamic web of interconnected and inseparable energy patterns. In this theory, the traditional concepts of time and space, of isolated objects, and of cause and effect no longer exist.

Holding this view of the universe, the occurrence of miracles becomes not quite so miraculous. The wave pattern changes in the physical world, or in an individual's mind or body, may cause or be the result of energy or wave patterns elsewhere in the universe.

Many of the Eastern religious philosophies combine the essence of the scientific theory described above into a mystical religious setting. These beliefs generally state that the entire universe is made up of a single essence, which might be called God, Prana, or Life Force. These philosophies further state that we are continuous with each other and with everything that was, does, or will exist. We share a common mind, and the differences that we perceive between ourselves are only illusory. This mystical approach again brings us back to the oneness of the universe, and this system readily explains miracles to a large proportion of the world's population.

These miraculous occurrences can now be described as *within the laws of nature* or *not within the laws of nature*. It is all the same. Some call them coincidences, blessings, accidents, flukes, strokes of luck, healings, or miracles. These explanations present a spectrum ranging from the approaches of modern physics to the spiritual approach of today's religions.

Now perhaps we can understand how an individual or group, through their prayer, intent, or dynamic thought processes, can create an event so unbelievable it becomes classed as the miracle that it really is. Taking this one step further, one can see how miracles of circumstance can occur as one's energy patterns mesh and interconnect with all other energy patterns in the universe. We think about someone we have not seen for years, and he or she almost immediately calls on the phone, lost objects are found, two people meet in a distant land and their lives are changed forever, water may turn to wine, or the Red Sea may part.

And is it not possible that there is truly an *intelligent creator* of all things, and these mechanisms put forth are just how this intelligent creator operates our universe?

As to the why of miracles, the answer seems less obvious. In my own life, each miracle seems to offer a lesson: its presence bringing some new level of understanding to my life's journey. Perhaps we cannot clearly understand the significance of events as they unfold around us in each moment. Yet, over the course of time, I can't help but sense that these events are part of a larger dialogue, a conversation if you will, that a living and intelligent universe seems to be having with its inhabitants. Call it a *divine creator* or simply the impersonal mechanism of some mysterious force; either way it is hard to miss the sense of peace and awe we feel when for a moment or perhaps longer, we feel connected to something much bigger than our usual selves.

Chapter 41
Perhaps a Glimpse?

In 1999 my ninety-four-year-old mother, Tillie Harris, died. One might say that she had lived a very fulfilling life. But the immediate events that occurred at the time of her passing gave me pause to wonder about what might possibly be after what we have labeled as death. She had been living in a residential care home for some time. Her health began to fail during her last year of life. She suffered from a variety of physical symptoms, mostly age related. And she had become increasingly despondent as she became more and more dependant upon caregivers for her everyday needs.

One evening at about six o'clock she remarked to her caregiver, "I am ready to go now." The caregiver did not give it much thought and had not reported it her family. Then at about three o'clock the next morning, by the caregiver's account, she sat up in bed, and exclaimed, "I've changed my mind. I am not ready!" Those were the last words she ever spoke. She fell back, dropped into a coma, and died two days later.

Why did she speak those words on that morning? My own personal conjecture was that someone or something spoke to her and said perhaps something like, "Tillie, it is time." I told this story at her memorial service. As I have said elsewhere, I have come to believe that every so often, in somewhat unpredictable fashion, we are handed a free lesson. We can write off this event as just a coincidence, or take it as lesson about life and death, and learn from it

Chapter 42
Three Remarkable Events

S ometime in 1978 I was concluding a business transaction with an associate who, as the result of that transaction, had owed me a large sum of money. He was about to make the final payment on the promissory note that he had signed years before. He quite reasonably asked me for that promissory note and that it be marked paid in full. Easier said than done. The note was stored somewhere in cartons of papers that had to do with our business venture. I had not seen that note for at least five years. After hours of searching, I quite offhandedly said aloud, "God, please help me." I walked over to the desk that I had used hundreds of times since signing the note, and there it was, neatly folded and right on top of all of the other things on the desk.

As a professional healer, I was called upon to visit a woman who, on examination by an ultrasound study, was discovered to have lump in her breast. That discovery was made on a Friday, and she was scheduled for a needle biopsy on the following Monday. On the weekend days following the ultrasound, the woman and I, through prayer, guided imagery, and energy healing, did work to repair whatever pathology might be present. When she presented herself for the biopsy on Monday, which was attempted by two different physicians, no pathology could be detected. She did mention to her physicians that she had done some prayer and healing work over the weekend, but they continued the painful probing with biopsy

97

needles. Eventually they suggested that she return in three months for a recheck. To date (ten years later) there has been no recurrence.

Another time, in the early eighties, a rather severe pain awakened me in my upper abdomen. Not wanting to believe it could be serious, I talked myself into the fact that it just must be an upset stomach. But the pain persisted and finally I was taken to the hospital by one of my family members. My physician told me that my cardiac enzymes were elevated and my EKG indicated a severe cardiac problem. I was admitted to the coronary care unit of the hospital, and orders were given to sedate me because of my pain and anxiety. When the nurse came to administer an injection of Valium, I refused. My words were something like, "I have work to do and I cannot do the work if I am unconscious." After about twenty-four hours of intense self-healing or imaging (in fear, I might add), my doctor could no longer detect any abnormalities in my EKG and my lab tests had become normal. I was discharged to go home. They never did figure out what had actually happened to me, except that perhaps the results of the lab tests and the EKG might have been in error.

And so what is the significance of my three remarkable events? Well, for one thing, these are just the tip of an iceberg of remarkable events that have occurred in my life. Many writers have described similar cases. But these events were very personal. They happened to me. My own thoughts on the subject are that these and many other events in my life have been given to me for a reason. I have come to believe that these are just a few lessons of how things really are. In all honesty, I was never a believer in anything that could not be scientifically proven. When lecturers and writers spoke about the unity of the universe and some sort of underlying intelligence, I was pretty much turned off.

However, when I think of someone, and then they call me, or I run into them, I have to pause and wonder, "How come?" And there are other times when I wonder about a particular question, and at the very instant that I ponder a question, the answer comes over the radio or in a newspaper headline. As a searching, questioning human

being, I feel that I must rethink my former need for *scientific proof.*
These lessons seem to come in unpredictable fashion, but usually at
the time that I do most need that particular lesson.

It is much too easy to write off these events as coincidence. And
if we do this, I believe that we have denied ourselves an opportunity
to learn more about what I have come to consider the *underlying
intelligence of the universe.* Some call them miracles. I have come to
believe that this is just how things are. It is my belief we should
accept these lessons, learn from them, and let them help us in how
we govern our lives.

Chapter 43
Wait Until the Sun Comes Up

Have you ever noticed how often the emotional pain of anxiety and life's normal worries can be greatly magnified after you have gone to bed at night? And this can often cause you to lose a night's sleep.

When you are troubled by the happenings of life at night when you are trying to sleep, sometimes it is nearly impossible to shut off your mind. Around and around go the thoughts (usually negative). Dozens of thoughts of *what if's* or *what shall I Do's* bombard your brain.

I have learned in my own life that these horrific goings-on of the night usually gain the perspective of reality after I awaken and go on with my normal daily activities and experience the light of day.

I am not saying that the seriousness of any issue should be ignored. I am just saying that if I am able to talk to myself when those crazy thoughts seem to engulf me that everything will usually appear differently the next day. Actually sunlight has been shown to have antidepressant qualities.

If you can, use this self-talk device. As a result, you may be able to get a night's sleep, which you may not otherwise have had, but perhaps more importantly gain a more realistic perspective on the problem at hand.

Chapter 44
What Really Matters
Perspective on Life

I was watching a documentary about the earthquake that occurred in San Francisco in 1989. Many survivors were interviewed. Some of those who were sifting through the wreckage for some semblance of their former lives spoke a common theme. And that was that *things* did not matter anymore. It seems that their entire perspective on life had changed after this most traumatic event. For these survivors, it seemed to come down to what really matters.

What I found most surprising is that the people who were interviewed about their change in focus in their lives were of a broad range of ages, from young adults to older people. From my experience, our culture of materialism pushes us, especially at younger ages, to achieve and to acquire.

But why is it that when we lose or are threatened with the loss of everything that we may finally notice what really matters in our lives? Perhaps it is because we become wiser and more aware with the passage of time. This kind of perspective can occur with an endless number of events ranging from the loss of one's physical home, recovering from a potentially deadly illness, loss of a loved one, to some cosmic experience.

Things as referred to here are the material objects that we felt were essential before what could be described as a major change in perspective due to a life altering event.

Certainly for most of us, whatever financial abilities are required to maintain a reasonable standard of living (paying rent, buying food, and so on) are not unimportant.

And *things* are different in everyone's life. To a homeless man, the cart that he pushes his belongings around in is a *thing,* but it is truly essential to his survival. To the young successful entrepreneur, a new shiny BMW may be a *thing* that he believes he could not do without. But could a catastrophic and traumatic experience level the playing field? There are no absolutes in interpreting what may be *things* in people's lives.

What might be the goal of this change of perspective? It would be different for everyone, but I believe that it might be to achieve a level of peace that may not have been present the one's life prior to the life-changing event.

What I am suggesting is: Why wait for a traumatic, life-altering event to occur? As wisdom is acquired, it may be time to look within and reevaluate one's priorities, and then perhaps in one's life, to move in the direction of what really matters.

Chapter 45
Laughter
The Least Expensive Medicine

It puts a smile on your face and costs nothing. Children laugh at one or two months. Primates have also been shown to demonstrate laughter. It can heal anger. Imagine being mad and laughing at the same time. It lets you be a child again, and lets you take off your grown-up costume. Laughter is contagious, and you can catch it whether you want to or not. Laughter is an instant vacation. It is the shortest distance between two people.

And what is so neat about laughter is that it is fun. It can be a bonding factor in families. It can actually heal relationships. Imagine what a benefit it would be in a marriage if couples could laugh together instead of stressing out together. And believe it or not, it is dietetic in that one burns more calories laughing then when not laughing.

Laughter reduces the level of stress hormones like cortisol and epinephrine. It also increases the level of health-enhancing hormones like endorphins. Laughter increases the number of antibody-producing cells and enhances the effectiveness of T cells. All this means a stronger immune system, as well as fewer physical effects of stress.

So what is my advice? Take off your straight jacket. Loosen up. Respond to humor, or create it. Observe children and animals. Appreciate everyday humor; notice the comical things that happen around you. Spend time with people with a sense of humor. Have fun. Life is short. Enjoy yourself.

Chapter 46
Forgiveness
A Way to Peace

I was speaking to a woman recently who mentioned to me that she is unable to hold a grudge. She said if she really tries, she can hold a grudge for, at the most, one day. What a gift, I thought. What a wonderful way to find peace in one's life. It seems that forgiveness will most likely never be an issue with her since, at the very most, one day after an event, any emotional energy connected to that occurrence is gone

Forgiveness is a process by which we release ourselves from the pain that we have experienced at the hands of others. And the good news is that forgiveness is optional. It is not something that we do for other people, but rather something that we do for ourselves so that we can get well, move on with our lives, and free ourselves from the continuation of pain and anger. It is a gift to our own peace of mind and self-esteem.

It does not mean that you agree or condone what others may have done. That event cannot be erased. What is done is done. But you can release yourself from being *owned* by that event. A famous writer, Ann Landers, described hanging on to resentment as letting someone that you believe has wronged you live rent-free in your head.

At times the inability to forgive, and even perhaps to seek revenge, can literally eat you up alive. One's sense of what is just and fair may handicap one's ability to forgive.

Letting go of resentment and animosity can make way for compassion and peace.

Present day medical research has shown that holding anger and bitterness can lead to a chronic stress response in one's body with increased blood pressure, decreased immunity to illness, and numerous other possible health issues. In this frame of mind we are also more prone to depression, anxiety, and chronic pain, and at much greater risk of alcohol and substance abuse.

In most instances the optional process of forgiving may be accomplished, but forgetting what happened may be impossible. This does not mean that benefits of forgiveness should be overlooked. In relationships, forgiveness can often allow the relationship to continue, whereas otherwise it may not survive.

Perhaps even more difficult than forgiving others is forgiving ourselves. Practically none of us have avoided making missteps in our lives. Often we hold ourselves to impossibly high standards. However, we are human and subject to all of the human frailties. How often have we said or done things that created real damage or ill feelings with others. There is a rule in our culture and in life, and that is that most of the time you cannot take back your words once they are spoken. However, you do have choice of sincerely apologizing if you choose, and hopefully for your own mental well-being, the apology will be accepted.

At times the process of deciding to forgive can be a difficult. The violating event may have occurred many years ago, and the offender may even be deceased, but the thoughts and feelings of it still crowd your mind. It is a conscious process whereby one must ponder the advantages of forgiveness and determine if it is best course of action for one's own mental well-being. From my experience, it usually is.

As a therapist, I have seen the miracle of this process in my clients and in my own life. My advice is do not overlook the possibility of the gift of forgiveness and what it might do for you.

Chapter 47
Put on the Armor

Definition of armor from *Wikipedia:* A person's emotional, social, or other defenses: his armor of self-confidence.

Perhaps one of the most important qualities required for success in our society is self-esteem. However, this quality can become quite fragile at times, especially if one is assaulted verbally by another, be it your boss, your mate, or anyone else. This means when you suspect such an assault may be forthcoming, you need to literally *put on your psychological armor.* This means there is no need to acknowledge or react to the assault when you know who you really are. The assaults just bounce off of the armor. Perhaps it is the one doing the assault who has the problem.

However, if this assault is sprung on you before you have time to don your armor, then do some examining of the event after the fact. How really valid is the assault and who is this person that dares to attack you? Perhaps he or she has the problem. Most often with this after-the-fact examination, you still come out the winner and your self-esteem is not damaged.

For parents this whole concept is extremely important. Your young child will probably not have sufficient self-confidence to question his or her parent's words, and the child may take it all in, whether valid or not. Be very, very cautious with your words when correcting your child. Positive reinforcement is much more effective than a negative assault.

Chapter 48
Change the Channel
A Path to Positivity

How often have you slipped into what I would call a *funk*? This is a very *down place* for which there is no immediate explanation. We all do cycle through a variety of moods in our lives, but this funk can literally flatten us and can put any form of happiness on pause. It can feel at times like a temporary depression as one's mood spirals down. Perhaps it may be time to *change the channel*.

I am not referring to changing the television channel, but what I am referring to is about changing your *thought channel*. The plain and simple truth is that our thoughts govern our lives, and believe it or not, we do have control over our thoughts. It can be done, but it takes doing and remembering to do it. I have used this expression of *change the channel* in dealing with clients with a variety of emotional problems ranging from depression to OCD (obsessive compulsive disorder). This expression seems to be more effective than asking people to change their thoughts. This might be because we often use this expression with reference to television.

There is a form of therapy that has been found to be one of the most effective. It is called Cognitive Behavioral Therapy (CBT for short). Through this form of therapy, we are taught to change our negative or self-destructive thoughts to positive thoughts and thereby change our feelings and our mood. By this means, as our lives get better, the whole process becomes self-reinforcing, which allows a pattern of positive thoughts to become a habit.

You do not need to see a therapist to use this method. It is there to use, if you have the determination to do it. The following is one of many tools that can be used to precondition one's self to use positive thoughts to get you through a rough spot in your life.

This tool is called anchoring and it is a device by which one can *change the channel* in advance. Find a quiet place or room where you can relax and do the following imaging. Think of a time in your life where you were feeling great. Imagine this time with all of the sounds, colors, and feelings that you can bring up. When you totally immersed in this event, squeeze the thumb and middle finger of your right hand. Then clear your imagination and repeat several times. When negative thoughts overwhelm you, squeeze the same two fingers, and the pleasant memories you created will sweep over you and release the negativity that seemed to engulf you in the moment.

Another aspect of this whole process is the effect thought has on our lives in a completely different way. Much has been written about the power of positive thinking. It is about how one's thoughts can actually change one's physical world. Doors can be opened and events can be caused to happen in a truly physical way. I am not just referring to psychological events.

Bottom line, watch and monitor your thoughts. If you find yourself dwelling on less than positive thoughts, *change the channel* and see how your life will change. This may take constant vigilance. It really works.

Chapter 49
The Gift of Appreciation

The definition of appreciation as described in *Webster's Ninth New Collegiate Dictionary*: a sensitive awareness, a recognition of aesthetic values, an expression of admiration, approval, or gratitude.

Appreciation is a word, or perhaps better a concept, which when expressed can create joy or warmth in another. To be appreciated can also have the same emotional impact as a genuinely meant *thank you.*

Appreciation is a powerful and all-too-often unused tool for bonding people. We all like to be appreciated. I find in my practice as a therapist that perhaps the most common denominator beneath whatever reason people seek psychological help is low self-esteem. And this most often comes from a childhood where the child does not receive approval, and there are no indications that the child was truly appreciated.

To express appreciation for another can be an incredible gift, and it does not cost a penny. And on the other hand, to be the receiver, an expression of appreciation can change the flavor of one's day or one's life.

This expression can have an impact in so many areas of our lives. In a marriage or relationship, the true expression of appreciation can heal wounds. It can change the flavor of a work place when an employer expresses appreciation for the work done by an employee. So very often we might forget to express this powerful healing tool, perhaps because we may not realize what a gift it can be to another person.

And it can be done in so many simple ways. Expressions such as "Good job done" or "Thank you so much for your effort" are simple and free to extend.

There are other areas where I think appreciation would apply. We all have had challenges in our lives. This is just part of being alive. But sometimes these challenges, whether they are physical or emotional, are so overwhelming that we think we will not survive, and then we may see someone with far greater challenges. Hopefully we can then appreciate that there are people far worse off, and we might appreciate what we have and may have the courage to move on.

Another perhaps delicious part of the concept of appreciation is that we, ourselves, will be able to appreciate a beautiful sunset, the miracles of nature, perhaps the warm sun on our backs, or just waking up in the morning and being alive. Certainly there are endless levels of appreciation to be experienced outside of ourselves.

And certainly, and not finally, the concepts of appreciate, appreciation, and to be appreciated lend an incredible richness to our lives that otherwise may have never existed.

Chapter 50
To Be There for Another

O nce in a while there may be people in our lives who, more than anything else, simply need someone to be present for them, to share in their fears and their suffering. Lost in their own pain, they may yearn to be listened to in a truly empathetic fashion, to be truly heard, and to feel less alone.

There may also be times of joy, when they miss the company of another, someone with whom to share the happy events of their lives. We are social people by nature, and so often we just want another person with whom we can share the experience of life.

When someone is reaching out to us, it can come in many forms. It might be a phone call from a friend, or a fellow worker who opens up to share something real about his or her life. It might be the look of pain on the face of someone that you encounter, or a startlingly honest response when you extend a caring, "How are you?"

It can be an incredible gift for you to be that person who is willing and capable of lending the support so badly needed by another. Often when one's troubles go unexpressed, troubling thoughts can just go round and round in one's head, magnified by loneliness. Sharing with another can be extremely therapeutic, even liberating.

There is an effective mode of therapy in psychology called *the talking cure*. This is exactly what we do when we are there to hear and truly listen to a person in this process of just being there for him or her.

This need to connect deeply can be present in any variety of relationships, ranging from marriage to friendships or even with a desperate stranger. Our ability to recognize that need, and then be able to step forward to be deeply present for another, is a vital quality that can affect every relationship in our life.

As a therapist I have often seen this in couples' relationships. I have seen men who work hard to accomplish and provide for their families but, at the same time, are not able to be truly present for their partner when needed. Yes, for sure, women are different from men and have different emotional needs, but I have noticed that men are at times oblivious to the emotional needs of their female partners who be need to be heard and understood on a deeper level. Perhaps feeling that their role as a provider is enough, some men fail to develop the empathetic listening tools that might be needed to heal a wounded connection with their partner.

I would say to these men: If things are not working well in your relationship and your partner appears troubled or distant, take a close look to see if you're really being emotionally present for her. Are you listening quietly when she expresses her pain or her joys to you? Do you acknowledge what she has shared and help her to feel heard and understood? Are you able to hear what might sound like criticisms without overreacting? Develop the courage to talk to your partner, and see if perhaps her unfulfilled need is for you to connect on a deeper level. This may be what stands between you.

And what is the role of those who choose to be there for another? First of all, it may be just to be there, to be quiet and present and to listen. Amazingly, that in itself is usually enough. Often the person in need does not require advice or fixing. He or she only needs to be heard. But there may be times when his or her helplessness does seem to cry out for advice. Simple as it seems, validation may be all that is required.

Yes, it can be a challenge to be able to step outside of one's self to be there for another, but your reward will be witnessing the positive difference that your presence may have made in another's life.

Printed in the United States
By Bookmasters